The Healing of the Waters

THE HEALING
OF THE WATERS

Poems by
AMOS N. WILDER

---

*And he went forth unto the spring of the waters, and
cast salt therein, and said, Thus saith the Lord, I have
healed these waters; there shall not be from thence any
more death or miscarrying.*

II KINGS ii, 21

WIPF & STOCK · Eugene, Oregon

Wipf and Stock Publishers
199 W 8th Ave, Suite 3
Eugene, OR 97401

The Healing of the Waters
By Wilder, Amos
Copyright©1943 by Wilder, Amos
ISBN 13: 978-1-62564-639-2
Publication date 4/15/2014
Previously published by Harper & Brothers, 1943

COLLEGIS DISCIPULISQUE

IN DIVINITATE

SERIES FOREWORD TO THE
AMOS N. WILDER LIBRARY

GIVEN THE SUPERFLUITY OF books in the world, there has to be a compelling reason to reissue those that have gone out of print. Most often a curious reader can rely successfully on interlibrary loan or Google Books to gain access to what the publishing world has otherwise let drop. But this piecemeal retrieval is not sufficient when an author, rather than a single volume, warrants being brought back into circulation; when there is a whole body of work deserving of a fresh audience. Such is the case with Amos Niven Wilder (1895–1993), whose prodigious writing, spanning the better part of a century, claims our attention with its extraordinary variety of genres (poetry, essay, and memoir) and disciplines (biblical study, literary criticism, theology).

First, the man behind the publications. A gift for writing and a passion for literature were very much in the family's DNA. Named for his newspaper-publisher father, Amos was the eldest of five, four of whom distinguished them as writers. Most famous of them was his only brother, the playwright and novelist Thornton

Wilder, about whom he wrote "Thornton Wilder and His Public" in 1980. Educated at Yale University, from which he eventually received four degrees, he also undertook biblical and theological studies in France and Belgium but most importantly at Mansfield College, Oxford, where he encountered the likes of Albert Schweitzer (*The Quest of the Historical Jesus*) and C.H. Dodd (renown for the notion of "realized eschatology," wherein the end is not near but now). These years of schooling launched his career as a distinguished New Testament scholar at Andover-Newton Theological Seminary, the Chicago Theological Seminary and the University of Chicago, and finally at Harvard Divinity School. Yet perhaps more crucial to his personal development than this academic training was his service in World War I, during which time he served as a volunteer ambulance driver in France and Macedonia (receiving the *Croix de guerre*) and later saw significant action as a corporal with the U.S. Army field artillery in France. That the "Great War" shaped his life and career is suggested by the works that bracket his publications: his first book, a collection of poems, *Battle Retrospect* (1923), and his very last, *Armageddon Revisited: A World War I Journal* (1994). Both bear witness to a traumatic wartime experience that neither destroyed him nor ever let him go.

For many, the trenches marked the end of faith, but not for Wilder. Upon his discharge he went to Yale Divinity School, was ordained in the Congregational Church, and served briefly as a parish minister in New Hampshire. By the end of the 1920s, however, he was back at Yale to do doctoral work in the New Testament.

Impelled by a fascination with eschatology, that branch of theology concerned with "last things," he focused research and imagination on traditional themes: death, the end of the world, and the ultimate destiny of humanity. But this was no antiquarian theological interest; it was his way into a deeper understanding of the Gospel and the times in which he lived. It is not difficult to connect the academic study that culminated in *Eschatology and Ethics in the Teaching of Jesus* (1939, 1950, 1978) with the trauma of World War I; it is even easier to understand why throughout his career he was drawn to the apocalyptic literature of both Jews and Christians. In France he had been inside an apocalypse, had felt the earth reel and rock, had seen the foundations of the world laid bare (2 Sam. 22: 8, 16). It would not do to dismiss these biblical visions, as many did at the time, as surreal and grotesque fantasy; they were, he would argue, grounded in an actual Armageddon he had witnessed firsthand. "Reality" as it had been known before the world had been torn open for judgment. It was time for revelation.

The correspondence Wilder saw between ancient apocalyptic and the experience of his own generation—between notions of biblical crisis and the revolutions of the twentieth century—inspired an already established biblical scholar to become a literary critic as well. Turning to texts sacred and secular, ancient and modern, he discovered in them a common situation, what in a 1971 essay he called "nakedness to Being," an "immediacy to the dynamics of existence." When you live in a ruined world, you must study the ruins. Literature was a place to begin.

iii

He began, in fact, with the particular literature of biblical writers: parable, myth, apocalypse, and Christian rhetoric in all its forms. Moreover, rather than travel the well-worn, dusty paths of the New Testament academy, Wilder invested himself in an exploration of biblical imagination at a time (unlike the present day) when few were doing so. What precisely was the world the Scriptures asked us to enter, and how did language bring it to life? Parable and apocalyptic were especially compelling to him as they emerged, he argued, from "a crucible where the world is made and unmade."

Wilder did not approach the Bible "as literature," but rather as the Word of God articulated in a variety of literary forms. He welcomed the new attention being paid by literary scholars to the Scriptures—Northrop Frye, Robert Alter, Frank Kermode—and was grateful that windows had been opened "in an ancient library long obscured by stained glass and cobwebs" (as he wrote in an endorsement of Alter and Kermode's *Literary Guide to the Bible*). Yet he was not uncritical of what they found on the sacred page, nor did his interest in literary theory prevent him from arguing against the Deconstructionist notion that biblical narrative (*pace* Kermode's *The Genesis of Secrecy*) was finally indeterminate and open-ended. For Wilder, the Gospel of Mark, for instance, was "too urgent for puzzles and mystification"; it was not a cryptogram but an "opening and crowning disclosure" of glory.

In a daring move for a "guild" scholar, even one long drawn to questions of biblical interpretation, Wilder also opened his readers to the poetry, fiction, and drama of the twentieth century. An early foray into this career-long exploration was *The Spiritual Aspects of Modern Poetry* in 1940; a decade later came the decennial Bross Prize-winning *Modern Poetry and the Christian Tradition* (1952), *Theology and Modern Literature* (1958), and then *The New Voice: Religion, Literature, and Hermeneutics* (1969), where he touches on novelists (Proust, Gide, Sartre) and poets (Eliot, Robert Lowell, David Jones). These books invite the theological reader to be at once nourished and challenged by twentieth-century literature. However, the were written not only to expand the horizons of biblical scholars, but also to develop an interest in religion among those not inclined to seek it out. Still more ambitious is Wilder's 1976 book, *Theopoetic*, with its call for a renewal of biblical religion itself through the cultivation of the imagination. This required the risk of the new, stepping beyond the safety of the familiar and time-worn to explore deeper waters: "Old words do not reach across the new gulfs, and it is only in vision and oracle that we can chart the unknown and new-name the creatures." Before the message, came the vision; before the sermon, the hymn; before the prose, the poem. (He began his life as a writer in 1923, after all, as a Yale Younger Poet.)

Wilder's *The Bible and the Literary Critic*, published in 1991—just two years before his death in his 98th year—offers his own retrospection on a life's work spent on a border between Scripture and literature, proclamation and critique, God's Word and the poet's new account of everything old. Thanks to Wipf & Stock's republication of his works in "The Amos N. Wilder Library," we now have a chance not merely to look back on an extraordinarily varied creative life but to realize anew what it stands to offer our future explorations of the Bible and its literary afterlife.

Peter S. Hawkins
Professor of Religion and Literature
Yale Divinity School
New Haven, CT
October 2013

CONTENTS

vii

ACKNOWLEDGMENTS

The author wishes to make acknowledgment to *Advance* for permission to reprint here two of the poems included; to *Christendom*, similarly, in which three of the poems were first published, including "The Chant of Creation"; and to *The Christian Century* which first published nine of them. From *Battle-Retrospect* in the Yale Series of Younger Poets, 1923, now out of print, five poems have been reprinted, including the "Ode in a German Cemetery" and "The City of Man", formerly entitled, "Lines by Arno." From *Arachne: Poems*, 1928, also out of print, the following have been included here: the sonnet sequence, "Annals of Circumstance and Beauty," in a revised form; "Visions by the Lake of Orta," likewise in a revised form; and ten shorter poems. The poems from these two volumes are reprinted by the kind permission of the original publisher, the Yale University Press.

The Healing of the Waters

THE CITY OF DESTRUCTION

Paris, Boulevard de Clichy, August 1939

And the men of the city said unto Elisha, Behold, we pray thee, the situation of this city is pleasant, as my lord seeth: but the water is bad, and the land miscarrieth . . . II KINGS ii, 19

And there came two angels to Sodom at even . . . And they said, Nay; but we will abide in the street all night. GENESIS xix, 1, 2

They did eat, they drank, they bought, they sold, they planted, they builded; But the same day that Lot went out of Sodom it rained fire and brimstone from heaven, and destroyed them all. LUKE xvii, 28, 29

THE vision of the streets,
The vision of the city,
The vision of the generations;

One city, all cities,
Babylon, Tyre,
Jerusalem, Rome,
The city of man,
The City of Destruction.

.   .   .   .   .

They throng on the boulevards,
They press by the tables,
They overflow on the pavement,
They loiter, they assemble, they pass.
The surges advance and are broken.
The multitude drifts,
The welter of waves has no end:
This stream of this gulf of the ocean of man.

From center and faubourg,
From every quarter,
Both young and old
Take their place in the concourse,
Issue from by-streets,
Emerge from the Métro.
They teem at the corners,
They weave and they mill.

They spy out diversions
And gloat upon rumor,
And gather in knots
Where voices are raised,
Where mischance befalls,
Where mischief is mooted,
Where heads may be broken,
Where blood may be drawn.

They compass about
The kiosks and the stalls,
The purveyors of news,
The criers of ill-tidings,
Alarm, defamation,
The tribunes of slander,
The fliers of faction,
The banners of schism.

They mass at the doors
Of the temples of chance,
The lottery booths,
They kneel at the rail,
They commune at the comptoir,
They snatch at the lots
And fight for the numbers,

They elbow their way
To the racing affiches,
And devour the despatches.

They stream in and out
Of the cinema caves
Where a phantasmagoria
Is cast on the night;
Where, bloodless and jaded,
They borrow of life
From flickers and fictions;
Where echoes of passion
And shadows of impulse
Move in their minds;
Where hammered by violence,
Needled by sadism,
Scalded by pungencies,
The illusion of power
Flatters their nullity;
By galvanic shocks
Convulsed for an hour;
By spectral transfusions
Alive for a season.

They pass down the by-ways
Where street-lamps are dimmed
And the house-fronts are blind,
The notorious quarter.
Bolts slide in their grooves,
Doors shut and are opened,
There are rustlings in portals,
Procurers at corners,
Invitations in whispers,
Provocations in shadows,

Perfumes and sorcery.
These are her mazes,
The concession of Astarte,
Where Circe spreads her banquets,
And love flaunts her arcana,
Where the soul is aspired
In the pit of the senses,
The funnel of Hell.

They compass about
The wrestlers, the clowns,
Marionettes
About marionettes,
Scenting out scandal,
Avid for victims,
Famished for calumny,
Fainting for blood.

.   .   .   .

The watchman on the roof,
His clarion mocked;
The prophet in the bazaar,
Reviled by the doomed;
The angel in the street,
Jostled by the damned.

.   .   .   .

For they beckon destruction,
They draw the avenger
With cart ropes and cords,
Defying the Furies,
Deriding disaster;
A city insensate,
They shout on the housetops,

4

They sit down to drink
And rise up to play,
Their hearts overcharged
With banqueting, surfeiting,
They curse in the alleys,
They reel in the gardens,
And say, Let us see it!
Ay, let it draw nigh!

And the foe asks no better,
His hordes are in motion,
The archers are prompt,
The horsemen are instant,
The chariots thunder.
The city has summoned
The ram and the mortar,
The fiery shafts,
The swordsman, the headsman,
The horrible rector.

And the Lord said,
The cry of the city is great,
I will go down now and see.

And I stood in the garish streets at nightfall,
In the last days of the city,
While the earth trembled
And the air grew sulphurous,
And convolutions of livid smoke boiled up from the
        neighboring crater;
Electric tensions played
And a strange glare lighted the faces of the living dead.
I passed through the Carnival,

5

Jostled by the masquers,
And I heard the execrations and the blasphemies.

And I halted where the ways cross,
Facing the oncoming throng,
Memorizing and devouring those faces and those forms,
As Dante and Vergil halted in Malebolge,
Confronting the scourged torrents of the damned,
And like them I beheld malice wedded with woe,
For judgment foreruns judgment
And destruction sends out its angels before.
For here were new forms of penalty,
Unsuspected plagues and new fashions in anguish,
New engines and demonries,
And new imaginations in agony;
And the tormented were the tormentors,
And the harriers the harried,
Sinned against and sinning,
And the victims were the guilty.

And I saw the streaming throngs of the city,
Infected, riddled, pocked and blistered—
A basket of figs, very bad, so bad they cannot be eaten—
A people with fatal legacies,
A race with a fatal inheritance,
A cloth eaten by acids,
Charred by withering fires;
And all these souls agonized as men are agonized
By the forethought and the afterthought,
The review and the anticipation,
Stretched in a torture chamber of solicitude,
In the exquisite torments of conscience
Where imagination raises all to the infinite scale.

And in that circle whence, if report be true,
None ever return alive,
I saw familiar forms
And recognized ancient offenders;
Branded as aforetime, and with the well-known insignia,
And the tell-tale gait and gestures,
Themselves and their progeny:
All indeed the sons of Adam, with his harrowing visage,
With the image of God in eclipse, and the countenance
    darkened,
But darkened diversely,
And the daughters of Eve with her troubled demeanor,
But troubled diversely.
Thus, Cain with his brand and his sentence,
Solitary in the concourse of his brethren,
And at bay amid the indifferent.
And Ishmael, hating and hated, for every man's hand is
    against him.
And the builders of Babel, the crass, untaught by their
    ancient effrontery,
Avid and febrile still to pile up storey on storey
And show themselves insolent against the Almighty.

And Potiphar's wife and her kind, idle, unyoked,
    disencumbered,
The wanton daughters of Zion that walk with mincing steps,
Their vacant hours given to the arts and rites of their beauty:
Unguents from the perfumer and kohl at the apothecary.
At home they pore upon mirrors and glance aside into
    fountains,
Fretful and gnawed by dalliance.
They linger at the doors, they twitch the curtains, they sigh
    at the casements.

I have decked my bed, saith she, with coverings of tapestry
    and fine linen from Egypt,
I have perfumed my bed with myrrh, aloes and cinnamon,
For the goodman is not at home, he is gone a long journey.

And I saw the wretched son of Shimei who goes cursing,
Unconscious of the throng, pale, and muttering with
    paranoid intensity,
Who holds to life by this, whose ecstasy is his hate,
And whose song is his malediction.
How opened for him these poisoned wells?
And where runs the network of these channels of venom?

And I saw the dwarf of covetousness,
With the scorched soul and the febrile pulse;
He betrays himself in his ways: he is so conscious of the one
    thing he is unconscious of all else,
And unwittingly he presents himself as the fool.
So often and so long has he pored on the images of chance,
Gloated on the images of aggrandizement,
That he is less now a man than a lust.
He is a dedicated spirit as devils are dedicated,
And so dedicated that he has offered up father and mother,
    brother and sister, wife and child, sunlight and
    starlight.

And I saw again the damned soul with the lascivious squint,
Hawking the ways and conveying his solicitations,
Beating the thickets for his game,
Adept in appraisal,
Pastmaster in the sleights and cues of his commerce.
He moves enveloped in the images of lust
And feeding on the secret hoard of lubricity,
And his eyes are full of adultery.

This plague is more instant and consuming than those of the
     body, though it goes before them.
His gaze is on the central crater of Hell.
This is a fountain that gives forth iniquity continually and
     of the most ancient.
Here man's nature is uncreated from of old.

I saw moreover the reluctant and surprised child of wrath
     that had betrayed the woman
And stumbled on inklings of that wherewith he had to do;
For out of fatality the soul speaks,
And in the hour of treachery as in the hour of death the
     innocent are august;
And he goes with eyes darkened and a brand on his brow,
And a sound of terror is in his ears.

And I saw the insensate and fatuous mother
Who not only stood in the fire but led her youngest children
     with her;
And the unweaned babe with the mystery still on its face
Wheeled at night through the infernal streets
Where the fiery flakes of malediction whip the recalcitrant
     and drive them to fury.

So the glare of Hell played on the city,
Its fissures open in the streets,
Its fumes frenzy the multitude,
Its lavas rise in the heart
And its fiery particles lacerate the flesh.

     .   .   .   .

The oracle of the streets,
The oracle of the city,
Nineveh, Babylon, Tyre:

9

One city, all cities,
The Cities of the Plain,
The city of man:

Up, get you out!
Escape for your life,
Look not behind,
Neither stay in the plain,
Flee to the mountains
Lest ye be consumed,

When the earth opens up
And engulfs the blasphemers,
When sulphur and brimstone
Rain from the heavens,
When the windows of heaven
Are opened and the living
Are whelmed in the waters
And choked in the deluge.

.   .   .   .

O Lord, cast a branch into these fountains that they be
    sweetened.
Cast salt into these springs and heal these waters
For the water is bad and the land miscarrieth;
Let there not be from thence any more death or miscarry-
    ing.
O Lord, sterilize these ancient roots of ill;
Quench these perennial fires.
Allay these coursing fevers,
And bring us from these transports into thy peace.

DOOM

(After Isaiah)

THE age is febrile and beside itself:
  Ridden by ten thousand passions, unawares
Fallen on alienation; 'tis a house
By seven disastrous demons dispossessed
Who hold unreckoning carnival and trade
In dyes and linen and the souls of men.
The generation is adulterous:
Its vows abjured in hoarse rapacity,
Its faiths all sponged in truculent despair.
It runs on heartless courses, and pursues
Insensate quests and strange obsessive cares.
This people is accursed and knoweth not
The law, but plunged in brazen cecity
Calls peace what is not peace and darkness light,
Shouts on the housetops while the parapets
Crumble and fall before the battering rams.
Too soon the chariots roar about the streets,
Too soon the incendiaries fly like fiends
With torches in the alley-ways. Alas!
The palaces, the ivory summer houses,
The cedar work and gay partitions blaze;
And of the temple stones that housed the Presence
No longer one upon the other left.

UNSHRIVEN

They have not known the quiet we have won,
The silence we have entered into here
Through all the exiles of this many a year,
The insensate cares that led us hither and yon.
They have not known the pardon that has fallen
Upon us from the wronged, magnanimous past,
The plenary indulgence that at last
Composed these hearts that once were vexed and sullen.
They have not known the peace that we have known—
Therefore forgive their folly and their rage,
The strange obsessive fevers of the age;
The love we know, alas, they have foregone.
They have not known the quiet we have won
Nor seen the Face that we have looked upon.

TO THE GOD OF DELIVERANCES

Thou who art far greater than ever we have explored
    Thee,
Whose ways far outrun our query,
Whose thoughts are deeper than Hell,
Whose devices are unimaginable
To compose our chaos,
To resolve this anarchy
And to lead out unsurmised gain from this our capitulation,
(For we are but turbulent dreamers,
Larvae on the first steps of being).

Thou who dost yet perfect that which concerneth us
And move us, unwilling, whither our deepest will aspires;

Thou whom our truest conceptions so diminish,
Whom our most daring intimacy so finds yet so removes,
Sierra of the soul.

O Thou who remainest silent,
Whose heaven is as brass
When continents in sanguinary delirium blaspheme against
    Thee;
Yet shall not God avenge His own elect which cry day and
    night unto Him?
Yea I tell you, He will avenge them speedily.

And thinkest thou that the Almighty made this great scheme
    of things for naught!

For that silence withers all blasphemy,
Withers all sophistry and craft of men;
Against that court of silence every lie falters in terror.

Thou who remainest silent,
Thine answers being so swift
That speech were far too tardy for Thy vindications.

O Thou who art far greater than we know Thee,
Prayer unto Thee! We thirst!
Prayer to those with Thee enheavened
There where the wings of the soul beat less vainly—
Pity for the sons of men,
For these that blaze in the long ecstasy, the long torment,
    of consciousness,
Unconscious of God,
Burning, burning, burning.

Pity on these Thy little people,
On these who amid the darling possessions of the meek,
The tiny and fragile paradises of the poor,
Know only the brutalities of chance,
The mattock of that boor, Fortune,
The violations of the proud.

Pity for changing mortality,
The vain generations
Below the horizons of Golgotha.

It was not Thy will that man should come to naught.

O Soul of man,
Breathe life through all the members
From Thine eternal home within.
Nay, stand forth among us!
Pass once more through these shades that Thou hast cast
    forth
That they may know their nature and now at last awake.

TO PULPIT AND TRIBUNE

SPEAK holy words—too many blasphemies,
  Too many insolent and strident cries
And jeers and taunts and maledictions rise.

Speak faithful words—too many tongues that please,
And idle vows, and disingenuous pleas,
And heartless and disheartening levities.

Speak quiet words—the constellations wait,
The mountains watch; the hour for man is late
Likewise to still his heart and supplicate.

Speak chastened words—for anguish is at hand,
Intolerable, that none can understand,
And writs of ill no mortal eye has scanned.

Speak gentle words—for fallen on the knives
These sentient hearts and these exceeded lives
Bleed till their pitying Advocate arrives.

Speak holy words—and O thou tarrying Lord,
Leave not thy cherished to the power of the sword;
Come with thy hosts and rout the opprobrious horde.

THIS DAY

This day is a day of trouble, and of rebuke, and of contumely; for the children are come to the birth, and there is not strength to bring forth. ISAIAH xxxvii, 3

Shall I bring to the birth, and not cause to bring forth? saith the Lord. ISAIAH lxvi, 9

As though our world had never seen the thorn
Bear at long last the unimagined rose,
As though our kind had never seen the morn
After a night of storm its pomps unclose;

As though no selfsame testimony ran
From clan to empire and from clime to clime:
"The inscrutible gods pursue their cryptic plan,
An unthought fabric pays the cost of time;

Some undreamed crystal marks the ancient throes,
Some breathless temple stands above the tide,
Some arch of peace atones a myriad woes,
Some coral ridge stands when the seas subside."

As though the tumbling mountain masses ne'er
Broke into altitudes of glistering snow,
As though the endless, calcined desert bare
Ceased not amazed upon the ocean flow.

O wait upon the ancient miracle
Ever renewed; discount the eternal boon!
Feel through these years some tide of purpose swell,
Otherwise great, now in the world's mid-noon.

These infinite tasks are portents of a Work
Afoot among us toward transcendent ends;
Behind these ruins and these hungers lurk
Strategies unsurmised and secret trends;

And once again our world shall see the bud
Of patience burst in miracle of bloom,
And once again our race shall see a flood
Of sudden grace irradiate the gloom.

SO IS IT

So is it here on earth:
  We serve transcendent ends
Blindly; our deed transcends
These shows and brings to birth
Effects beyond our dearth.

So is it among men:
Our iron circumstance,
Weakness, and the advance
Of hours that bring again
Frustration and mischance;

And yet these strivings blind,
This travail and this pain,
Are tissue of some brain,
The cell-work of a Mind
That waxes as we wane.

Our blind toils are the cells
That build a higher being
To see beyond our seeing,
And in our bondage dwells
A virtue for our freeing.

HOMAGE

To T.N.W., 1942

To those who offer themselves willingly in the day of
   decision,
In the great arbitrament,
Who are prompt at the gate,
And who present themselves foremost at the fords of
   Megiddo,
And take their stations at the narrow issues:
Theirs are the great jeopardies, the necessary role, the
   memorable name,
Their encounter is with the heart of darkness.
For some the searchings of heart, the scruple, the fastidious
   witness,
For others the fateful evasion, the abiding reproaches,
For many the frivolous and the usual occasions.
But these on the crumbling levees match themselves with
   the infuriate flood.
These beneath the waves toil at the primeval sea-walls
Whose courses were laid against chaos.
These repair the moles erected of old against the ravining
   deep.
These descend where the nethermost piers of history are
   building,
And place their lives if need be at the foundation of all the
   ages of glory to come.

ON THE REPUDIATION OF WOODROW WILSON

November 2, 1920

For that our fathers sowed the slopes of time
   With seed of faith that still its harvest yields,
For that they called him Lord to whom the shields
Of all the earth belong, our latter dearth
He overlooked, Who brings all things to birth,
And led us to the eternal battle-fields
Where through the ages His own sword He wields
To prove us worthy of our country's prime.
Now we indite the temper of that hour,
Now we abandon the unburied slain,
In panic at the unwonted light we cower
And stampede to our midnight ways again
While plead and clamor for that glorious morn
The suffrage of the dead and the unborn.

ODE IN A GERMAN CEMETERY

Where Many Fallen in the Great War Were Interred

RANCOUR grows chastened in these groves of death,
And clamorous recrimination hushed,
  Our pain disarmed by pain,
We can but leave upon these graves the wreath
Our mortal foes by mortal visitation crushed
  Have woven for their slain.

  Still to this day,
Driven by their bitterness, they come to pray
  And kneeling in the grass
  Grope vainly for relief,
    And as I pass
Rise in distressed confusion and sore grief.

What did these know of empire's devious ends,
Markets and routes and ancient rivalries?
Balance of power and dark expediencies,
    Reasons of state,
The vain hallucinations of the great?
  Why should these make amends
    For others' wrongs?
What guilt for all this ruin here belongs?

Muse on these mute inscriptions, each of which
Stands for a life past divination rich
  In poignant exploitations
  And eager explorations
Of its allotted freehold in the Day;
Rich in those naive essays of the heart,
  Forlorn, confiding gestures

That of this dark enigma make assay,
  And tendril-like adventures
Whereby we grope and sound and prove
Whether or no some hidden Love
Greet and reward our motion to aspire.
  Muse on each acted part;
Forgotten exultations, rage, and smart,
  Their faith's extinguished fire,
And little triumphs that none think upon,
And protests smothered in oblivion.

Muse on this epitaph that meets the eye,
Strangely familiar in its unknown tongue:
  "These for our homes did die,"—
Two brothers loved of nameless folk, who won
This as earth's final comment at Verdun,
In that stentorian month whose havoc flung
Its hundred thousands down to Acheron;
  In that inordinate reaping
  Of these our fields beneath
When twilight was congested with the hosts
Of death's dim, swarming envoys bent upon
Prodigious inroads down life's fertile coasts,
  Its virgin prairies sweeping
In far incursions where no scythe had shone;
Till earth was cumbered with the oppressive weight
Of such a garnering underneath the sun,
  Such high-heaped sheaves of death;
    Till one by one
Borne off across the stars in phantom state,
  Death's groaning wains conveyed
The great ingathering to the realms of shade,
And throngs unwonted choked the Stygian gate.

. . . Races of men, co-heirs of earth's duress,
Children of night, and orphans of the void,
Ringed 'round with menace and with mystery,
Condemned at birth to death in loneliness,
Proscribed and hunted, trampled and destroyed
By the blind furies of the earth and sea;
Why thus increase the overwhelming odds
Against us—add this self-inflicted curse—
That we should hunt each other in the path
Of cataclysm, stay to vent our wrath
One on the other in the middle-way
Of swift annihilation, tear and slay
Beneath the onslaught of the universe,
Wage civil war, our seats stormed by the gods?
E'en the wild beasts forego their lust for blood
Fleeing in panic through a blazing wood. . . .

Mysterious is the lot of common lives
    Lost in the mass,
Anonymous as leaves or blades of grass
In the thick verdure of humanity,
And inexistent to the powers that be.
    Such were these all;
    And so like leaves they fall,
        Or one by one,
Or, when some storm of retribution drives
Over the face of mankind at the call
    Of surcharged passions,
Unnumbered from their humble holdings wrenched,
    Before the blast they run,
Creatures of life's blind impulse and its altering fashions,
To the deep drifts of still oblivion;
    Save where their thought survives

In that sequested spot where they were known,
In some frail fort of love 'gainst death and time entrenched.

Even their vices were not all their own,
    Inevitably sown
In childhood's hospitable tilth
    By the thick-flying seed
Of man's continuing legacy of ill,
His cherished heirlooms of disease and filth,
And rank depravities of ancient date,
And unimpaired inheritance of hate,
That generation unto generation still
    Contrives to will.
Errors, obscenities and passions breed,
    With germs of violence rife,
As in a culture fitted to that end
    In human life,
Nor need man to their breeding his impulsion lend.

    Then, fallen foe, and friend,
        Sleep,
        Sleep in repose,
And you, you suffering mother, cease to weep.
    What though we late were foes?
We fought in nightmare, as in dreams we live;
    Best to forgive.

Aspiring howsoever, you, or I,
The great world weaves its tentacles of ill
Into our hearts, the solidarity
Of mortal evil claims us 'gainst our will,
And with it sinning, with it we must die.

Yet those who in the world-old process caught
Bring thither self-renunciation, aught
Of loftier aim, of loftier ideal,
        Of loftier thought,
And bear the common curse, the shared ordeal,
The common retribution, undeserved,
These in all lands, all times, all causes, these
        That law by innocence appease;
By their sublime attractiveness they win
The world from its fatality of sin,
        And from the common lot
        Desiring no exemption,
Their blamelessness with mighty power is fraught
        When joined with pain,
        For so Redemption,
Redemption lifts its mighty cross again!

        So swerved
By love's vast leverage from its ancient grooves
And changeless cycles of eternal wars,
        The planet moves
To grander revolutions among softer stars
And skies unblasted by the beams of Mars,
To placid periods under milder rays,
Pacific seasons, august nights and days.

Munich, July 1921

25

PRAYER WITHOUT WORDS

S AY not a word, be still, and fear to pray;
   Forego not the great prayer of silence; plead
With the great plea of helplessness, and say
   No word but vast dependence for thy creed.

This impotence is thy best title; this
   Ebb of the spirit calls to all the seas.
The eternal travelling waters of the abyss
   And of the height know all their estuaries.

This is the last resort, the ultimate claim,
   The plea that cannot fail when all has failed.
The heart whose prayers are mocked, that in the flame
   Itself is charred or shivered, here is healed.

"AND WITH NO LANGUAGE BUT A CRY"

I HAVE a heart that cries to God
Abandonedly across the blind
Imperfect avenue of mind,
I have a heart that cries to God.

I have a heart that cries to God
Across the quarried stones of thought,
The labored temple slowly wrought,
A heart, a heart that cries to God.

I have a heart that cries to God
Immediately and must dispense
With faltering through the world of sense,
And calls across the mind to God;

That calls across the worlds to God,
Nor stays to elaborate the tongue
Of sacrament too slowly wrung,
I have a heart that cries to God.

DE PROFUNDIS

Out of the utmost pitch of wilderment,
   Out of the stunned distress of ignorance,
Amazement, laceration, and despair,
The offering trampled, the derided ardor spent,
   Deliver us, O Lord,
And make thy power our truth, our sight thy Word.

From consternation's stroke, and the last hope
Bereft, and darkness' shattering scimitar
Counselling madness, and the palsied stand
Of those who in the noontide totter and grope,
   Deliver us, O Lord,
Fed from thy secret manna's hidden hoard.

From the blanched visage of affright, the soul
Smit with the rod of horror, tasting so
Creation's *culs de sac* of death, and black
Relapses of the species from the destined goal,
   Deliver us, O Lord,
And set our souls the effulgent issue toward.

From dreadful death, the wasting and the fire,
Corruption, and the obscenity of decay,
The torture of mad thoughts, and conscious course
Of dissolution in sin's viewless pyre,
   Deliver us, O Lord,
With bread of health from life's abundant board.

"DALL' ORRIBIL PROCELLA IN DOLCE CALMA."
—MICHEL ANGELO

I WOULD know mercy from the supernal calms;
I would know benediction and the balms
    Of the ultimate persuasions;
The unguents of the marble tomb, the night
Of death—its suavity and blest evasions,
The sudden space! the fragrance, and the starry flight.

There like some mariner from raging seas
And wastes chaotic past God's boundaries
Who issues on some halcyon reach, some floor
Of crystal, round a headland, while the roar
And carnival of storm behind him dies;

There in the elements' benign suspension,
There would I oar the breathless firmament
        In calm ascension,
        Released, unspent,
Trampling the aether with the eternal plumes
        Of exultation,
    Fanning those chambered glooms,
Lavender twilights, velvet far oblivions,
        With noiseless pinions
To some divined, remote angelic station.

INTERCESSION

YE merciful angels! fend these quivering hearts,
And interpose, O God, thy merciful shield
    For these exceeded souls.
Immure in heavenly safety, blessedly sealed
From bludgeon'd grief and all pain's furious darts
    All thine o'erdriven souls.

Gather in providence about these heads
Sacred with pain, benignant ministers!
    Henceforth forever turn
In wreaths of calm where fiery gledes and cares
Revolved, and present stings and future dreads,
    There ever wreathe and turn.

Enfold these spirits in love's ample skirt
Compassionate Christ! that stoop'st among the stars,
    Environ them in thee;
Bereave of laceration, tears, and scars,
Nay, give thy glory and indue their hurt
    With thine upon the Tree.

DAILY BREAD

THIS daily bread, these unexpected crumbs,
   This sudden bounty here and there that comes
To anoint the eyes and to regale the heart:
O woo these gifts and choose the better part.

The inspired instant makes whole hours glow,
The genial impulse sends its overflow
Through arid stretches, and the flash of spirit
Irradiates the darkness we inherit.

This bread of life: some facet of a soul
Ingenuously displayed that shows the whole
Of human charm and poignancy; some spark
Of nascent understanding; or the stark
Rebuke of human anguish on earth's stage;
Some apparition of forlorn old age,
Infinite compunctions in our thoughts to breed
And stir us from the slumber to the deed.

Such daily bread of intimate communion
With hurt or joy or eagerness, this union
Of pilgrim beings in a veiled abyss,
These hails across the sea, the wilderness,
Enlighten the eyes and magnify the heart —
O woo these gifts and choose the better part!

THANKSGIVING

Be our daily bread withheld, be it given,
  Thanks for the bread from heaven;
Though on sense disease and pain come stealing,
  Thanks for the spirit's healing;
Thanks, when the springs of impulse are defiled,
  For the renewing candor of the child;
Thanks, when the years sully the face of truth,
  For the resurgent heart of youth.

Thanks, though we be cast off, unknown, alone,
  Thanks that we are well known,
And though our outward man and lot decay,
  The spirit kindles day by day;
Thanks that our sorrow by thine alchemy
  Turns out to be the very fuel of glee,
That from our utter penury, we bless,
  And having nothing, all things still possess.

Thanks for the faith that sees beyond these snows
  The clemencies of God, the lily and the rose,
Beyond these graves, these ruins and this waste,
  A garden of men, an empire undisgraced;
Thanks that each loss we own, each death we die,
  Calls out of heaven amazing ministry,
Thanks, thanks that the costly travail wrought in dearth
  Shatters old worlds and brings new worlds to birth.

CHRISTOS LOGOS

Δι' οὗ καὶ ἐποίησεν τοὺς αἰῶνας

HEART of the world beyond the gleams of day,
O ardent sense, deep, deep in the life of things,
      Deeper than day and night,
Deeper than flesh and all time's shadowy rings,
Deeper than death, thou core of all, thou stay
      In the eternal night.

Thou corner-stone of the uranian nave,
Axis and center of wide being's girth,
      Thou polar star of souls;
O Cross pitched at the navel of the earth,
O spectacle this side, that side, the grave,
      O cynosure of souls!

O flaming heart from whom all kindlings start,
Impassioned dreamer of the universe
      Whose splendid impulse runs
In crimson floods of glory to immerse
And fill the ocean reaches of the heart
      Under its setting suns.

Spirit that moves in the unfathomed pit
Of thought, thou ghost in the aghast abyss,
      Haunter of mystery;
Conception darkens in us thence, and this
Thy mind is dark imagination's seat
      That broods on verity.

One life thou art in splendor and in love:
The face of naure takes its veil of dreams
      From heaven's holiness;

An effluence of beauty sets and streams
Athwart the world from pity pierced above,
    Whence every loveliness.

Through thee the worlds were made. It is enough:
One heart gives utterance in many forms;
    Or in the firmaments,
Or in the face of man, or in the storms
Of earth's successions and the laws thereof,
    Or reason's governments.

ALIVE FOR EVERMORE

Whom God hath raised up, having loosed the pangs of death:
because it was not possible that he should be holden of it.
ACTS 2:24

HIS spirit lives; he died and is alive,
That pure will haunts this guilty world forever.
How could men's idle fury drive
That mighty shepherd from his sheep? Or sever
His heart from Mary's, Peter's? Or deprive
Iscariot and the thief of his blest rod,
Far in the ultimate night apart from God?
Never, never
Could death's thin shadows dim that ardent Sun!
He walks amid the Golden Candlesticks
Today, and lights all souls while time shall run
Who on the tree by his own troth affixed
Has knit the life of God and man forever.

THE SON OF MAN

Thou child of man; thou birth of a travailing people;
  Thou resurrection from a crucified race,
That through the blood and outrage and despair
Of faith's encounter with flesh and circumstance
Conceived Thee in relapse on God and failure:
Ghost of expiring Israel in an hour
Estranged and alien: great Unrecognized,
Who brought with Thee to birth from Sheol's gates
Tending on Thee, millions of shadows strange,
Those who in martyrdom had fathered Thee,
Those who in suffering had dreamed of Thee,
From the intensest human had conceived Thee
Who most wert Man, who most art Man today:
Who shall but verge upon the mystery
Of whence Thou drew'st thy oneness with all flesh?
Yet in the black night of the universe,
Yet in the blizzards of eternity,
The towers of men upon a thousand plains,
The swarming hordes in desert or by sea
Are but as cowering sheep, a single flock
Huddled in storm. The son of Israel
Is son of Man, for Israel itself
Was son of Man, Man's truest-hearted child
To affront the unknown and wrestle with the dark
And call up from the unimagined depths
Of desperation of the human heart
The indwelling Spirit to make answer there,
For, as the aghast tragedian cried out,
Though there be things stupendous, strange, divine
In multitude—yet none so much as Man.

Child of a race, and child of nature too
Whose bloody ascension finds its type in Thee:
O only drama true to reach on reach
Of human scrutiny and tragic record,
Thou only correspondent, truest norm,
Most central figure, representative.
Thy cross stands at the center of the world,
Thy moment summed the million destinies,
And *millions of strange shadows on Thee tend*
For Thou art heart of hearts, the substance self
Whereof we all are made in time and times.

And from the subterranean granite depths
Of man's existence, to this surface life
Of history which is of least import —
Phenomenal — Thou once did'st rise, here too
In this convulsive web of consciousness,
This shadow-strife and interplay of shades
Under revolving suns and moons, to make
Thy sign eternal in our temporal scene,
And in the landscape of our chained events
And time's successions (which are but a form
From nebula to nebula) and play
Of mundane fealties, to show Thyself
As Thou art in the timeless, once for all.

We saw Thee, O Thou Lover of Mankind,
Thy gesture in the daily dust of life
Was lovely, awful, and inevitable.
The total dark transaction of creation
From Alpha to Omega, dark to dark,
Was focused in Thy motions, entrances
And exits, in sublimest miniature.

We saw translated to earth's hieroglyphs,
And in the phantasies of human minds,
And in the imaginations of our kind
What veiled, inscrutable, unhuman fact
Underlies Being, and eternity.
For all the fulness of the godhead dwelt
In Thee, in our humanity's conceit,
And we have light hence evermore to walk
And scorn the dark between the stars, and blast
The sphinx with our eternal understanding.

IN HIM WE LIVE

A THOUSAND fathoms deep our life is plunged
    In an exceeding plenitude of grace,
Its folly and its wretchedness expunged,
Its pity hallowed in Love's vast embrace.

Compassion like a flooding river brims
Along the canyon of the squalid street
Ample to lave and heal; and glory rims
The city skyline where dim pinions beat;

And pity like a tide engulfs the foes
Working each other havoc in the fray,
At worst the folly of children unto those
To whom a thousand years is as a day.

Love, that fanatic treasurer of hearts
Who prizes our beloved past our conceit,
Though circumstance converge on them his darts,
Shall fend their spirits in his close retreat.

There is a tenderness that bathes the world,
A peace that shelters terror in its skirt
And where the blind world's thunderbolts are hurled
Guards lest one hair of these dear heads be hurt.

The night is holy with an unseen Guest,
And with an august Lover sacrosanct,
Who stoops in care above the world's unrest,
Whose shining troop in host on host is ranked.

His condescension makes the night air sweet,
And music like a gust of fragrance blown

About our pain from unknown worlds does beat
Its strain of exultation in our own.

The authentic hope of which man grows aware
Reflects itself upon the sunset bars,
Man lends his pity to the midnight air
And presses his compassion on the stars.

THE NEW APHRODITE

How art thou wooed, thou sister of the Fair,
   Thou other Aphrodite whom men ne'er
By Paphos or Valhalla's marble stair
     Looked on appalled?
     How art thou called?

Unborn! Unborn! Sister of Christ arise;
Start from the wave of Europe's tragedies
Or justify Iona's prophecies.
     Columba's isle
     Awaits thy smile.

Messiah-maid, messiah-mother, when,
When shalt thou bring thy gentler regimen,
And consummate Christ's kingdom among men,
     And mollify
     Our cruelty?

What drama of redemption is thy part?
What basenesses of ours shall break thy heart,
And which of our Sanhedrins cause thy smart?
     What Calvary
     Shall we pass by?

How art thou wooed? How shall we lead thee home?
Daughter of Thetis and the ocean foam;
Eve unbeguiled, sister of Adam, come!
     Our evil dream
     At length redeem!

NOTE. *There is an old Celtic prophecy to the effect that the Messiah will appear in the form of a woman at the island of Iona to usher in the Millennium.*

THE CHANT OF CREATION*

When the morning stars sang together
And all the sons of God shouted for joy

THEY pealed and pealed and pealed, the bells, the bells!
In changing showers, in bursts that climbed and
    climbed
To touch the utmost reach of ecstasy
And fall, and climb again to higher ranges.

From deeps of joy such music wells and swells;
I heard the radiant changes
Pulsing and ringing hour after hour
All through the night, but from no earthly tower,
Borne upon other gusts than sweep these walls,
And with their proud ascents and dying falls
And glorious rumor—
As of exultant hosts that none could number
Thronging the gates of heaven in concourse dense—
Still to the ear of sense.

Joy there is somewhere past our hearts to hold,
Undreamed, untold;
Joy without name whose only voice is song,
And song unceasing like the waves that throng
And gather everlastingly and follow,
In mighty sequences that rise and fall,
Crest after crest and hollow after hollow,
From climax on to climax, and renew
Their radiant energy exhausted never.

* Schubert, C Major Symphony, Third Movement

42

And if day sever
From those majestic strains our halting march,
And that heaven-scaling fugue be lost to hearing,
And lost to sight the host that through the arch
Of the eternal triumph chanting moves,
Yet we the while abide their reappearing
And brood thereon, that all the hints and clues
We have of the ineffable conspire
To signify that death holds man's desire.

This music breathed so proud, so high a soul,
Proud unto suffocation, one that swept
From glory unto glory nor did tire,
Nor flagged nor felt the weight of wings, nor slept.
This music breathed so proud, so proud a soul.

He sang no personal triumph, his elation
Was strange and supernatural, a share
In that apocalyptic hour; stirred
By some excitement of All Souls, he heard
Phrases blown from that high transaction where
Through the wide portals of the consummation
Ten thousand times ten thousand and thousands of
        thousands,
A multitude from every nation treads
With everlasting joy upon their heads.

It is enough to know that in the bound
Of day and night such joy is somewhere found;
This universe gives hospitality
Beyond our view
In some unsounded depth to such felicity.
Provided such joy be

We whose whole gift of life is bounded by two breaths,
When our hearts cease to beat,
We can lie down and sleep our common deaths:
The song of life, the song of death is sweet.

All radiant be our aspect! O put on
Thy beautiful garments, Soul, and wear the fair,
The shining face of youth; move to this joy,
And tread like those whom crowding visions buoy,
Incredulous of despair.
Abide in this elation, ringed around
With these celestial confidants, exult
To hear the seraphic chorus sound.
In thy foreknowledge of the august event
Be jubilant
And glory in the unknown things to come.

We cannot dwell with sorrow evermore.
Those levels of dismay we shall not plumb
Henceforth; and they shall vanish like old lore,
Those dreams of ill, that old delirium.
Circles there are of the profounder pit
These feet have left forever; they shall range
On terraces with holier fires lit,
And for old prisons new expanses change.
Come blight, come reprobation and the play
Of time's most obtuse shafts, insanely sped
In some perverse election—far away
Beyond each tocsin or alarm of dread
We still shall hear, subdued although they be,
Those mounting carillons of victory.

This universal theme lives in the heart
Of Him of whom we are the shadows all,

Of Him of whom we take our better part,
And when the universe is still,
Listening upon the sill
And threshold of eternity, we know
Its rise and fall,
Within our dreams a heavenly overflow,
The chant of Him by whom the worlds began,
The ground-theme of the common soul of man.

This theme betrays Him and we know what mood
Exalted, deep and solemn bears Him on,
His reverie how tender and august,
And on what pinions
Of ever towering rapture unsubdued
He summons forth his luminous dominions,
Still adding dawn to dawn,
And noon to noon, and lifting cope on cope,
Expanding heaven on heaven beyond the scope
Of our aghast surmise.

And molding creatures from the sleeping dust
He breathes upon their ashen mouths, unstops
Their leaden ears with his forefingers, drops
His clay with spittle on their staring eyes;
They wake to nature and to more than nature,
He new creates each creature,
Folds in them wings they know not of to unfold
When all these present uses have grown old,
To lift them to His further flight on flight
Of being and His canopies of light,
His uttermost far tents
Of other natures, other firmaments.

They live a life of larvae, self-absorbed,
Blind on the very brink and shore
Of boundless radiance that they ignore,
Under mighty horizons drenched with light
And empyreans orbed
With sun on sun insufferably bright.

But on these creatures faithful to their clay,
Toiling beneath the dazzling blaze of day
In unaware transfiguration,
On these too faithful to their dust,
The heavens encroach in sudden usurpation;
The fashion of earth's vesture alters,
Glowing with strange effulgence, and a gust
Of music sweeps upon their blind endeavor.
A great light blinds
Their mortal seeing,
They grope at noontide and their footsteps falter,
They hear the paean of the eternal Son
Whose nature binds
All souls in one;
Charged with old tears it breaks into the minds
Of men from Him of whom they take their being.
The surging strophes mount and mount forever,
Till beyond time and death, past sun and star
They see the exultant concourse move afar,
Till beyond waking sense and lying dream
They know themselves eternal in that eternal theme.

ANNALS OF CIRCUMSTANCE AND BEAUTY

SONNETS

Alas! the endowment of immortal power
Is matched unequally with custom, time,
And domineering faculties of sense. . . .

                                    The Excursion

Dust as we are, the immortal spirit grows
Like harmony in music; there is a dark
Inscrutable workmanship that reconciles
Discordant elements. . . .

                                    The Prelude

DAZZLING and happy spirit, hidden away,
Lost in your own effulgence, do not stay,
Pause not upon what sombre threads are here,   *Proem*
What unblessed reverie or unhallowed fear.
Quell not your spirit with this sorrowful pall,
O from your lovely ardor do not fall!
This strain is ancient and each single grief
Was matter and fuel long since of ecstasy,
In many a crystal draught found its relief.
Since then, like Dante on the tiers of heaven,   *Io sentiva*
With the excessive glories I have striven,   *osannar di*
Have drunk from wells of peace and innocency,   *coro in coro*
Have seen the banners of the light unfurled
And heard hosannas ring from world to world.

FLOW back, flow back upon the amazed soul,
Flood of divine remembrance! From your sleep
Where vanished moons their spectral sessions keep,   *Evocation*
O vanished hours, rise to our day! Unroll,
Unroll once more the illuminated scroll
Of memory's golden legend from the deep   *Le soleil ne*
And bid its glowing evocations sweep   *peut rien contre*
Athwart the night of thought from pole to pole.   *ce qui n'est*
                                                     plus
So shall we learn what losses have been ours   *Valéry*
And count how many deaths the living die,
Note the divorce of souls for aye and aye   *O ombre vane,*
That, joined, had triumphed o'er the victorious hours, *fuor che nell'*
And mourning these lost loves and broken faiths   *aspetto!*
Know all for shadows and ourselves for wraiths.

WE PASS through worlds and worlds in sleep;
The pilgrim in the lowly inn

Transmigration   Bears no trace of the mighty deep
Nor of the spheres where he has been.
We pass through Limbos, and forget;
Impoverished of our shadowy lore
Of principalities that yet

Weigh me the   Glimmer, and powers we sense no more.
weight of the   For no substantial being is ours.
fire,
Or measure me   We glass the deep abysses blind,
the blast of   And there the flare of Tophet lowers
the wind,   Where late the Seven Candles shined.
Or call me again
the hour that   We traverse suns and moons in sleep
is past.   And guard no records of the deep.

BEAUTY prepares while lingering moons revolve.
Her gradual hosts foregather on many strands,
But not for us! O not for us! Dissolve

E che dirà nell'   In tears, Endymion, and wring white hands,
Inferno a'   You daughters of desire, alas, alas,
malnati: But not for us. The silver beacons catch;
Io vidi la spe-
ranza de'   We see the kindled tale of triumph pass
beati.   To peaks that past our dark horizon stretch.
Alas, O Follower, alas, alas,
You shall not know that City's ecstasy,
Its throngs' seraphic murmur. Glories mass
And gestate over continent and sea,
But not for us who reach our hands and pass,
The Unpermitted, O alas, alas.

IT IS not I who wrestle in these toils
  Of custom and occasion, O not I,
Not I, so scored and lacerated by
The day's indignities whose hurt despoils
The soul of its dominion and soils
With reek and blood its native majesty,
Nor is it I whose high serenity
Contumely stings, humiliation foils.
That is not I, or then if I it be,
How other from myself that view in trance
The eternal hour's immobility!
Froz'n in still beauty's moment that advance
Or passing knows not, but perennially
Shines, to annul outrageous circumstance.

*Circumstance
and beauty*

*The unfath-
omed existence
which riseth not
nor setteth,
where the ru-
mor of destruc-
tion reacheth
not, nor the
sounds and
echoes of re-
birth.*

  Bhagavad Gita

WE LIVE forever who one moment live
  In beauty's seizure; we may not go free.
Caught for all time in that captivity
The summoned spirit like a sphere doth give
Its reins to its compelling sun, and drive
In everlasting rounds, obediently,
Seized in her orbit and her harmony,
Forever driven, singing, and alive.
It is a dream that we should seem to toil
And suffer and rebel and faint and sin,
Bruised and tormented in this mortal coil;
No, no, our spirits are beyond this din
And there where hurtless fires all strifes assoil
Through long cerulean revolutions spin.

*The eternal
hour*

*Je touchais à la
  nuit pure.
Je ne savais plus
  mourir,
Car un fleuve
  sans coupure
Me semblait me
  parcourir.*

  Valéry

OMNIPOTENT confederate of all good,
Inexorable foe of all our ill,
Extirpate these bold motions of self-will,
Mortify these strange slips, the unblushing brood
Of vanities, and be thy surgery rude,

The invisible
world with
thee hath
sympathized;
Be thy affections
raised and
solemnized.

Until we wake to thee alone, until
All mild and disabused and meek and still
We pass with awe into thy plenitude.
So in an hour we have seen the face
Of nature change, and with our garish eyes
As though anointed with some lymph of grace
Seen common day grow solemn, as the skies
Foaming above with sable panoplies
Made of the world a hushed transfigured place.

If I beheld the
sun when it
shined, or the
moon walking
in brightness;
And my heart
hath been se-
cretly enticed,
or my mouth
hath kissed
my hand . . .
The Book of
Job

Le presenti cose
col falso lor
piacer

IF I have lifted up mine eyes to admire
The moon that walks in brightness on the hills,
Or kissed my hand to see the milky fire
That over sea and over land she spills;
If I have suffered my rash thought to range
About the greater light that rules the day
In impious scrutiny, or let like strange
Imaginations in my heart hold sway;
If I have been complacent to arrest
My gaze upon these things that do appear:
This bloom of flesh in which the soul is dressed,
Or said of art, "Behold what stones are here!"
O Thou who in Thy wisdom made all these,
Forgive the mortal's fond idolatries.

Bestridden by the gods and vexed to read
The dread foreshadowings of the strifes to be,
The Sibyl in prophetic agony
Knew no such rage as mine, nor extreme need
Of blessed utterance, nor to be freed
From such a weight and press of mystery,
Such rending talons of fell poignancy,
As when I heard your Promethean voices plead;
O Chopin, stormer of the gates of ruth,
Extortioner of tears, importunate
Of pity, who in exultation dost sweep,
And pathos, to invest the holds of truth,
To trumpet down the adamant of fate,
And coerce mercy from the unanswering deep.

Apollo and the Sibyl

Chopin

To create beauty in so dark a world!
And sing out of rejection and despair—
The bird astray in Hades whose song purled
There in the lava and the lifeless air—
Pitiful and sublime, in the deep murk,
This nether world without its sun or star,
Where cries resound and evil spirits lurk,
Here where the king of terrors is not far;
Something divine, here in so dark a place,
And blessed, to achieve a perfect act,
To lift such challenge to the realm of grace
From realms with torment and with darkness wracked:
In exile and estrangement, all forlorn,
To lift and blow Childe Roland's dauntless horn.

The thrush that sang in Hell

*out of rock,
Out of a desolate source,
Love leaps upon its course.
Yeats*

Grace in
disgrace

GOD loves the shabby hero and forlorn,
Sainthood in rags, and courage without means,
Grace in disgrace, royalty stable-born.
And history disguised in common scenes;
God loves humiliation and reproach

Thou hast
taught me
on powerless-
ness a power.
F. Thompson

Since Christ made every ignominy dear,
And Cinderella in her golden coach
Is not so graced as in her lowlier sphere.
God loves the poor man's riches ridiculed,

He fetters him-
self at every
step, and thus
gives his love
out in music.
Tagore

The flower in the tenement, the marred
And all pathetic gesture overruled,
The offering checked, the eagerness debarred;
God loves the furred hepatica that blows
Credulous in the latter winter snows.

BEAUTIFUL colloquy of voices, say,
How came the mortal on you? Where, and when?
How stole these suavities into his ken?

César Franck:
Variations
Symphoniques

Where had he wandered, whither did he stray?
O infinite sweet triumph, say, who pealed
These swift arpeggios, and these falling notes
Drenched in the pain of Paradise? What throats
Spoke to the rhapsodist in Sainte Clotilde?

But ye are come
unto mount
Zion . . . and
to the spirits of
just men made
perfect

He heard the pure and crystalline discourse
Of hearts that know now even as they are known,
Parleys of spirits made perfect and made free.
O rare evangel from love's inmost source,
Persuasive tongues of joy, what hearts of stone
Could long withstand your sheer felicity!

I saw a miracle beside the path:
  An apple tree in its first blossoming,
Absurdly small to lift against the wrath
Of Alpine brewings such a show, and fling
A spray, a snow, a burst, an incandescence,
A white éclosion like an angel's wing
Into this unknown scene; an iridescence
Of playing fires, the soul of the new-born,
Rioting in the open in the presence
Of Monta Rosa's menace; from some bourne
Of holy, fragile, jeweled, cherished things,
Unwarned, unapprehending, mid the scorn
And bludgeons of the hail-storm; how it brings
Rebuke of faith to our world's underlings.

Miracle by the Sacro Monte of Orta

From fevered crawlings o'er Siberian tracts,
  Rushes and faintings on the boundless steppes,
To issue on the silvered cataracts
Of the Pacific and direct one's steps
Along its moonlit gulfs and promontories
And overlook its dazzling pools; from blind
Phantastic toilings round the spiral storeys
Of hell's inverted cone to emerge and find
The stars again; from traffics to and fro
And shuttle ferryings within the mole
To thread some Indian archipelago,
Some endless Thousand Islands of the soul:
So was it at thy touch from my deep vein
Of dark conceits to glimpse the world again.

Convalescence

por lo inferno quaggiù di giro in giro

THOU art engraven in the bronze of thought.
Thy face is stamped above the swirl of time.
Thou liv'st forever and forever, wrought
At love's high noon, arrested at thy prime.
They are not all whose momentary flush
Of beauty on the adamant is limned,
Whose dead eyes burn, whose ashen cheeks still blush,
Alone of time's wronged fresco-hosts undimmed.
The million beings writhe like fumes of smoke
Beneath the dying suns on dying spheres,
And systems topple like the toppling oak,
Oblivion muffles the forgotten years;
But thou shalt time's vast overthrows elude
And smile in thought's immune beatitude.

*Pierre de
Ronsard to
Cassandre*

*Ephémère im-
mortel, si clair
devant mes
yeux . . .*
Valéry

THE scythes of time play havoc with the swarms
That breed and sicken on our dying globe
And shadowy harvests of unnumbered forms
Fall to the ruthless shafts that search and probe;
The circling moons put in their silvery flail,
Earth's gibbering phantoms flutter to the shade;
At last the moon's own lustrous course shall fail
And cinders strew the track the Pleiads made.
But thine unshadowed face shall haunt the gods
Embalmed in pity in the eternal thought,
And leap oblivion in those high abodes
To live anew in Edens newly wrought.
Then from this closing dark, O lighted face,
Bear record of me to that shining place.

*Shakespeare to
the friend of the
sonnets*

*Sovegna vos a
temps de ma
dolor*

*then remember
thy handmaid
I Sam. xxv, 31*

A cross the lost horizons of the years
     I hear sometimes the desultory guns
Trampling the midnight with a throb that runs
From ancient wars to strike upon our ears,   *The eventual*
Baying across the moonlit hemispheres   *peace*
Of dreams to bruit its thunders to the sons
Of days to come amid their benisons,
Their valleys unconvulsed, their tranquil meres.
No, no, the jar of sacrilegious war
Shall never shock that crystal atmosphere
Nor roll its angry surf upon that shore
With trepidation and the primal fear,   *Abundance of*
But till the moon in heaven be no more   *peace till the*
Abundant peace shall lock the magic sphere.   *moon be no*
                                                     more

L ove dreamed this place, it was not made by time;
     Glistening forever in its firmament
Of pure transparency—a glow unspent   *The Tomb of*
Poured from the imagination in the prime   *Ezra, on the*
And ecstasy of its conceit sublime;   *Tigris River*
Love dreamed these mirrored domes and palms, love blent
These hues and forms in its own element
Of floating glamor and its crystal clime.   *in questo miro*
It hangs there like some prospect of the soul,   *ed angelico*
Vanishing and abiding, as the arc   *templo, che solo*
Of heaven glows upon some drifting mist.   *amore e luce ha*
O magic passion whose serene control   *per confine*
So luminously shaped the formless dark
To leave us record of thine ancient tryst.

Logos

·

He the blind
Who weaves the
arches of the
mind
Shall granite
find . . .

Like pyramids
serene of ba-
salt, piled
Where with
hushed feet
move the im-
mortal gods.
Geoffrey Scott

THE signature of mind is on the deep
And thought has sunk its seal upon the inane,
And sudden fancies made incursion on sleep,
And flashes lightened o'er the night's domain.
Eternity shall hold the print of dreams;
Their subtle webs and filaments shall lie
Frozen in breathless climates in the seams
Of nature like some lost fern's gossamer die.
Form in the adamantine bastions, form!
Form in the crystal sphere, the triple bronze,
Form out of naught, to outlive with type and norm
Time's crawling insect-hill that slaves and spawns.
The soul is stamped on some Atlántean range
And silence chambers it above all change.

VISIONS BY THE LAKE OF ORTA

LET not harsh tongues do violence to this spell,
    Nor futile speech nor rhythms feebly borne,
        Nor song forlorn;
Music alone hath language in this vale,
And numbers like the tremors of a bell
        That swell and swell
Accordant with the tenor of the rhythmic morn.

    Against its crystal walls
    Our frustrate language falls;
Here needeth some diviner eloquence,
Some grammar won from angels and some word
Richer and ampler than we yet have heard,
    And some diviner sense.
If beauty be the element of song,
Itself a frozen music and a choir
Inaudible, so let me be the lyre
        To give thee voice
And to the world thine oracles prolong;
Bid thine inanimate praise in vocal song rejoice.

1

FROM THE SACRO MONTE

LIKE some quicksilver overflow, or some
    Blue writhing serpent, serpentinely sprawled
Along the vale, whose mailed limbs glisten from

NOTE: *The Lake of Orta, or Cusio as it was called by the Romans, lies in a deep valley in Piedmont to the west of Maggiore, and is dominated to the north by Monte Rosa. A Franciscan monastery and Sacro Monte are just above the village of Orta on the eastern shore.*

59

The triumphant sun, in molten beauty thralled,
See Cusio's lustrous firmament outspread,
Sparkling with lightenings and Alpine-walled,

With deep subaqeous springs pellucid fed
To take its every color from the skies
And render every tremulous image shed

On its invisible breast, and sympathize
With all its blue environing majesties.

Like some mirage of brighter atmospheres,
Richer champaigns and more translucent seas,
Somnolent isles in calm and radiant meres,

Like some mirage that we a moment seize,
Canvased in brilliance on our desert haze,
Displaced from distant climes by mysteries

Of cloud and heat, whereby we briefly gaze
On chases unpermitted and on shows
Forbidden, sacred and beyond our ways,

So liest thou in apparition that grows
More vivid momently and glows and glows,

Speaking of some lost world beyond the world,
Speaking of some lost sea beyond the sea,
Speaking of some remembered wave that purled

Upon a brighter strand perennially,
Of towers round which no ghostly clamors ring
And lives whose rounds are set to harmony,

Of hearts that cast the memory of the sting
And harrying of this world's delirium,
Pacing the cloisters of eternal spring

With buoyant sense, their fortunes overcome,
Tasting the fruit of mortal martyrdom.

Here let infirmity at length take heart
And here despondency itself grow mild.
Where such unearthly apparitions start,

Such shadowing on the Alpine reaches wild,
Such bright communications by the brink,
Where songs of unseen spirits reconciled

Re-echo, and where mortal eyes must shrink
And love so flame upon us from the earth,
Upon the words of *Beatricé* think:

A growing splendor where the soul knew dearth
Augurs the clearer sight and heavenly birth.

2

FROM THE TERRACE
OF THE MADONNA DELLA BACCIOLA

Here as I trod your hills, withheld, debarred,
And looked upon your lineaments in despair,
Finding them incommunicative, hard,
All unaware

I passed into the landscapes of the soul
And saw your waters in the mind of God;
Nor form nor hue but served the harmonious whole,
Nor leaf nor clod.

Divine imagination ruled the scene:
The transcendent artist, master of all form,
Had woven together on the mountain screen
The glooms of storm:

Color and shape and sound, odor and sense,
An infinitude of elements combined,
And, miracle of miracles, intense
With change, yet change to harmony assigned.

I stood and watched the eternal dreamer work,
Traced his creative act from hour to hour,
Whose canvases no rebel mediums irk,
Whose dawning thoughts upon the instant flower.

I saw the Alpine bastions ebb and flow,
And these so solid-seeming hills in rain
And sunlight, mist and glare, now gloom, now glow,
Melt and dissolve, reform and shape again.

Calmness grown visible, the balm of sight,
The element's self of sheer tranquillity,
The burnished mere—a filigree of light—
Raveled its shining hems perennially.

The toil of man himself was effortless
And full of silent music in that hour;
He moved as constellations, without stress,
He moved as conquerors in their day of power.

There far beneath me on the molten lake
I saw the boatman's bright oars palpitate;
I know not if I slept or was awake,
So perfect every trait;

And there that century-sombered tower below
Upon the oblivious isle that heeds no whit
Our coming and our going, nor doth know
Of us nor of these days that wash on it,

Unless by that same mood we enter in
Its medieval reverie, or grown
Contemporaries of the hills thus win
Their moment for our own. . . .

3
FROM THE SAME

NEW illustrations flame upon this glass
    Of nature's mind, new breathings and new jets:
These forms are beings, and their moods surpass

Our scope; though when the snowy cloud woof frets
The blue, or April's waxy leafage blows,
Or when the incendiary sun-god sets,

Or when with thousand fires the water flows
Or platinum blue beneath an inky sky,
We feel they are alive and do unclose

To the dread organ of the Phantasy
Intelligible language, wordlessly.

4

THE ETERNAL PATIENCE

HE guards it all in peace, this bosom of life,
This nest of nature keeps its constant sleep,
These mountain arms are patient round our strife.

Just so, a thousand years, these shadows creep
From bay to bay, oblivious of our wrong,
Just so from cloud to cloud the colors leap.

The heavens are faithful and the hills are strong,
The clouds return, and these deep seas remain,
Upon the slopes the woods forever throng.

To assault such bars of faithfulness is vain.
Our feuds surrender to these august faiths.
Beneath His lights our frantic torches wane.

His arms are round our tumults and our deaths,
His breath it is that stills our restless breaths.

5

LIKEWISE THE SPIRIT ALSO . . .
(On the Sacro Monte)

THE Spirit crying for eternal things—
Grieving for what it knows not, for a want
Without a name, and full of hungerings
For things beyond this tabernacle's wont.

The Spirit crying for eternal things
And charged with old rememberings;

Transfixed on ancient losses, and impaled
On the sharp barb of beauty and assailed
With all its mortal stings.

The Spirit cries; it knows what we ignore:
Some holier lot neglected, and some more
Radiant existence that we have put by,
Some scope or some communion we deny.

The Spirit grieving, dumb and deeply hurt—
This beauty, these wrought clouds, this pomp of light,
These swarming waters with their mountains girt,
These tones of bronze and this Franciscan site;
These mind the Spirit of its wanderings
And set it crying for eternal things.

6

SEQUITATEMI, O MORTALI*

*Wherefore, as by one man sin entered into the world, and
death by sin; and so death passed upon all men, for that all
have sinned . . . much more they which receive abundance
of grace and the gift of righteousness shall reign in life by
one, Jesus Christ.* EPISTLE TO THE ROMANS, V, 12, 17

The Christ speaks:

FOLLOW me, follow from this reign of death,
   O mortals! hasten from this hostelry,
This roof, this tavern of mortality;
Fly this phantasmal house,
Fly this fantastic breath.

* "Follow me, O ye that are mortal." On a seventeenth century fresco
on the Sacro Monte of Orta.

Denizens of this twilight tract whose eyes
Open upon a world whose walls are falling,
Fly these dark limbos filled with blasphemies
And plaints and outcries; hearken to my calling
Who bear the keys
Of death and hell and all the eternities.

Quit this dark shelf of being; fly, O fly
This sunken world, this tortuous gallery,
This alienated race.
Fly the malign miasmas of this place.
See where the flickering candle flares and drips:
Fly the immense eclipse!
Fly the impervious and the ebon night;
O fair, ephemeral faces,
Hasten your flight,
Follow upon my traces.

Through Sheol's deepest pit I took my way,
The labyrinths of ill I have traversed;
The gates of bronze asunder burst
And Abaddon hath yielded up his prey.
There in a desperate grapple death was foiled
And in the lonely silences despoiled.
Captive at length behold Captivity
And all the prisoners of the mighty, free.

Now through the world of flesh, the sensual scene,
Corruption's theatre, my word is spoken:
O race bemused, corrupted and undone,
The victory is won,
The spells are broken.
Rise from your deep obsessions, and behold,
On me the ancient bondage has no hold.
Henceforth I pass immune, the victory's got.

These withering fires, these vapors, clasp me not.
This furnace and these fumes have not so much
As passed upon my garments with their touch.
Me these distempers have no power to hurt;
Amid these turbid visions, sane, I see,
And in the whirlwind and the noxious gloom
Unmoved I go and come.

The poet speaks:

The whole world seeks to touch if but his skirt!

He passes through that carnival of ghosts,
Himself no ghost, substantial and self-ruled,
More real than them all; and mid the hosts
Of all the generations, all the lands,
This bright form mid the driven phantoms stands
And to earth's farthest coasts
Dispels their ills with his restoring hands
And quells their transports by his stern commands.

Man speaks:

He knows our lot:
Men in the flesh, yet living are we not;
Puppets of world-old passions, we but move
The tenements of untamed spirits that rove
From soul to soul;
And as he passes by
We shrink and cower;
Our bloodless demons recognize his power.
And some are won at his command, and rise
To look upon the earth with lucid eyes,

At length made whole;
And, when it is their hour,
Some in their spectre rage at Calvary
Think to affix their fear
And trample in a paroxysm of terror
Upon the truth that shines upon their error,
And with the idle insubstantial spear
To pierce the invulnerable heart of life.

The poet speaks:

But he eludes the ineffectual strife,
Him their distempers have no power to hurt.
We see his just eyes flame beyond the tomb,
The door being shut, he stands within the room.
Lo, all men seek to touch if but his skirt.
And to a world whose walls are falling
We hear him calling:

The Christ speaks:

Follow me, follow from this reign of death,
O mortals! hasten from this hostelry,
This roof, this tavern of mortality;
Fly this phantasmal house,
Fly this fantastic breath.

THE MARRIAGE TOKEN

WHAT token of love's everlastingness,
What symbol of an unattainted bond,
Of this sweet deep predestined care for thee,
Of this sweet deep irrevocable care,
What witness is sufficient for these things?
What gem or scarab, talisman or cross
May serve as charm in every lot or loss?

What stone immune to wear, pressed with the weight
Of mountain ranges, even as our hearts,
To an enduring hardness that eludes
The general cycle and the lapse to dust—
Exempt from weather, seasons and the rough
Abrasion of time? What amulet or gem
Could serve to bear and testify our faith
Securely in these unknowns we confront?

What ore, what element exempt from change
Fired in the unimaginable forge
In the world's incandescent furnaces,
Even as our hearts, to an enduring crystal
Patient of frost and fire, patient of flood,
Could yet avail to testify our faith
Securely in these fates that we attend,
These transformations that dissolve the worlds?

What pearl that wins its iridescence from
The beat of oceans and their storms of light,
Even as our hearts, what ripe fruit of the seas?

Such all are lost and broken, filched away,
At peril of every hap, without defense:

The child's bright shell, the treasure of an hour
Of the seas' splendor and the noon's bright story,
But lost, lost, vanished, stolen, swept away
By the days' flood, by the dark avalanche,
By the insensate billows, change and chance.

What band of gold that clings however close
To the sweet flesh, ay to the very bone?
What hidden pledge to hang upon the heart
Known to no other, intimate and dear?
What opal, onyx, amethyst or jade
Shall go with you securely through all fates,
What platinum survive these searing flames,
What crucifix dispute the unbodied shades?

Truly then were our love in jeopardy
Anchored thus precariously;
For it has need of deep pervasive powers,
It needs a guardian unattaintable
In floods and conflagrations, life and death,
Changes and chances here, and all the obscure
Onsets within the soul and mighty spells
Cast by malefic powers beyond our range.

Therefore be companied from this time forth
With that which shapes all crystal, rounds all pearls,
Lustres all gold and guides all craftsmen's hands,
Causes all flesh to bloom and knits all bone,
And gives us now to love and now to war
Mightily against every form of death
Or fear or sleep, infirmity or dismay.
Be fended, go inviolate, immune;
Our love pass, subtly armed, eluding all;
Fired, sustained, renewed, impregnable

By that which fires the worlds and moves the soul,
Ay, trust our love to that which gave it birth.

But reckon well the steps, the jeopardies.
My amulet of spirit now provides
For every ill and malady and shock:
The obscure fits of the spirit and the heart,
The blight cast on the future by past dearth,
The knowledge of what our love might have been,
Tedium, the aeons of unlightened skies,
Agony of the body and the soul,
The ineluctable doom on projects prized,
Frustration, year long disappointment, grief,
The halt of grace, hearts doomed to insuccess,
Love doomed to remain at length unsatisfied,
The heart-break at the penurious flow of joy,
The thunder-clap of open calumny,
Or long incomprehension, disesteem.

Yet bear and yet continue and yet trust
And yet be shielded, and return in hope
Again to that renewing well and fountain,
And lift your eyes to see the surf of clouds
Radiant on utmost horizons, skies beyond skies;
And listen to the throb of waves on shores
Beyond the darkest farthest promontories,
See where the white foam glimmers through the night
Silently upon undistinguished coasts;
Cast your hopes on to seas beyond these seas
Where we shall plough the furrows, lives beyond lives,
By other suns and other benedictions,
By other constellations, but all kindled
By the original fire that kindled love.

THIS IDLE HAND

THIS idle hand! let it have price with thee
For this, that it has lifted many a latch
And flung doors wide upon the earliest dawn
When earth was dim and cold and sacrosanct,
Has kindled fires in the world's dark night
And nourished dying flickers in the gusts
Of eerie canyons in the vale of death,
Has broken clods, and sown unlikely seed,
And husked the ears in snow amid the stubble.
This faltering hand, O cherish it despite
What tale of nerveless grasp or furtive sleight,
What jealous hoarding, may have palsied it
Past ample gesture or unreckoning stint.
Yet none the less let it have price with thee
For this, that it has raised the wounded's head,
And held their hand and steadied their vague steps
And borne their stretchers in the hurricane
Of storm and darkness on the marge of Hell;
That it has done the office of the heart
And of the priest to blind and lame and those
Distracted and the inconsolable;
And further, awful thought, hath broke the bread
Of that abiding Life and that pure Will,
And drawn with fearful love up to the Cross
These holy guests of earth, the children, there
To meet earth's holiest guest, the Child of God,
Whose human hand, for one, was true and wide
With largess for His kin, and therefore pierced.

MARRIAGE OF MINORS

BROTHER and sister in this world's poor family,
Jack and Jill out of this gypsy camp of an earth,
Here is where the injustice is greatest
And you feel it obscurely,
And you have a right to storm within yourselves
And seek sanctuary in one another's shabbiness.

This boy and girl with all their abandonments and futility,
Folly and dereliction,
Whirled from ignominy to ignominy,
Condemned to all the wretched chores of the community—
O tribute of forlorn humanity!
Come for his benediction whom they have blasphemed,
And somehow sense that they touch—what?
God, the Higher, all that they have missed:
Innocence and mercy and compassion.

Poor lad, scourged from humiliation to humiliation,
Pressed by dirt and danger, squalor and exhaustion,
And bred on blasphemy and the poison of men's bitter
        spirit,
And the maudlin imaginations of their lust;
Where else would it end but in this makeshift marriage?
And well may you storm within yourself, at the same time
        that you feel the awe of it.
God and the devil both have a hand in joining you,
And you are hardly at fault.

Poor sister in our earth's poor family,
Stupid and stupefied and hallowed all at once,
Poor creature of poor moments,
Disinherited Eve,

How else could it come out but in this tumble at the first
    assault,
And yet God has put his finger on even this.

No bridesmaids nor flowers for you,
The groom hasn't given you these.
You come in an old coat.
One of the gang is best man and witness.
The boy minister goes through with it,
And there is no shower as you go out.
The sleigh waits outside in the heavy snowfall.
It is movie night in the village, and no one is about to spy
    you at the parsonage,
And so you go off in the blizzard to the lumber camps.
This is all the world gives you.

But the Son of Man of the wedding feast haunts such
    occasions and understands you.
He can turn the water into wine and such shame and loss
    into gain
In some world some time.
Lucy Hanks bore Nancy seven years before her marriage
    feast.
The Son of Man knows too well what the hells are, and the
    dumb wonderings and sicknesses of the soul,
And he is the only one that does know.
So endure these gusts and whirlwinds of the night until the
    morning break.

I heard the organ roll behind the snowfall and saw in it
    the confetti of the heavenly bride chamber,
Glimpsed the sons of the bride chamber rejoicing
In that city which is full of boys and girls playing in the
    streets thereof,
Before the Father whose face the angels of little children
    do always behold.

THE MOTHER COUNTRY

As one who leaves his birthplace when a child
And grows, transplanted to another site,
All but forgetful of the scenes that smiled
Into those years a formative delight,
And then returns and strolls about the spot
And spies on his own infancy: there start
Dim intimations of the past, deep-wrought
Imperishable legend of the heart;
So the American that stands once more
On English soil where his forefathers stood:
Churchyard and park are half-remembered lore,
And shadowy recollections throng the wood;
The ancient rings lie ever at the core
And England's image sleeps in English blood.

IN A HAMPSHIRE LANE

*"He sendeth abroad his spirit
And the wilderness becometh a garden."*

"He giveth to each a body as pleaseth him."

THE thoughts of God are flowers, not graven stones.
We read his scripture on the flaming slope.
We see him dreaming where the fragile cup
Of scarlet swells precarious by the lane,
Unfolded moist and glossy from the lap
Of being, still to sacrosanct for touch,
Swollen with the blood of God to affright the earth,
A new flesh broken from the brain of him.

The thoughts of God are flowers; and we are flowers
(Save for the worm), and trees are flowers, and groves
And earth and sea and sun and stars are flowers:
The thoughts of God unfolding in the light,
Waxy and delicate and fringed with dew,
Blown like a miracle from nowhere, swaying
Consistent and substantial, taken shape
And form and body from the invisible
In flesh of satin and incarnadine;
The thoughts of God congealed in space and time.

And earth and sea and sun and stars are flowers,
Corollas limpid, iridescent, woven
In timeless looms, a gelatine of light,
An ethereal vegetation from the unseen,
Sprung in a night; the thoughts of very God
Thus apparitional in imagery,
Like rainbows sprung from nothing. Earth and sea,

Clouds, and the silver fires of night and day,
All are but petals and the flesh of flowers,
All are but bodies of an intenser pulse,
More fearful touch, and a more thrilling clay,
Uprisen within the meadows of God's dream:
Gigantic bells of color, blinding sheets
Of textured flame, cohering films and webs
Of radiance: the systems and the suns.

And we are flowers, immaculate as they,
Kin to the azure and the dazzling cloud,
The billowing green; kin to the ecstatic lark,
Caught up to all the freedom of the fields
Of space and all the sanctities of light;
Divine and marvellous in flesh as they,
Coursed by their impulse, fired by the same flame,
Tongues from the identical hearth, and likewise swept
By the identical breath of exultation.
Our little gift of mind divides us none
From forms insensate and the instinctive world;
A candle to our needs, it adds no joy,
Else could we carol as the skylark pitched
Against the woofs of storm that drive aloft.
And we are fellow to the impassive height,
Kin to the veering birds, the irradiate copse,
The bronzed grain (deep within whose shimmering sea
The poppies flame out when the sun appears)
Kin to the careering cloud and cloudlike earth.

And man is as a vegetation, a tract
Of marvellous foliage washed and drenched in dew,
Sprung of the sacred earth and purified
By wave on wave of beauty, tides of color
That sweep the visible earth. For when the breath

77

Of God inbreathes the world, the wilderness
Of man becomes a garden tilled and rich:
He fills the world's face with his cities walled
With providence and paved with righteousness.
His towers show like flowerings of stone
And God's thought blooms in pigment and in clay;
And the still song within the heart of things
That shivers in the bosom of the cloud
And chants in swaying beeches at the dusk
Escapes anew in rhapsody and praise
Of mortal tongue and mortal instrument.

TOURNAY

I MAGINATION smote me with his glaive
In Tournay's old cathedral as I stood
With holden eyes, and magic clapped his hood
Upon me, gazing down the vaulted nave;
I know not what impetuous angel drave
The garish phantoms thence and so renewed
The antique reverie, and the occult mood,
Cloaking me in the shadows of the grave —
Vistas I saw of arches without end,
The nether labyrinths of the Middle Age,
The catacombs of life, which high desire
Taught men by paroxysms to transcend,
Who so aspiring in ecstatic rage,
Transformed this prison to yon soaring choir.

SUNRISE ON THE HIMALAYAS

From Tiger Hill

Snows in the night loom in the sullen north
  Beyond an abyss of ridges brimmed with cloud;
Now fade in night's diaphanous eclipse,
And now loom forth
Out of the darkness' fluctuating shroud,
Conscious e'er night has run
Of visitings from the unannouncèd sun.

For these sublime existences ignore
The traffickings of India's darkling floor
And human lore,
And speak each other, beaconing afar
To sun and star
In speech untaught,
And hold a converse far above our thought.
Their language like an undulation leaps
Across heaven's steeps
And laps the headlands of the day and night
With storms of light.

Upon those faces vast
Invisible beams in night's obscurity
Break into milky radiancy;
There congregate white fires of the past;
The riotous stars have cast
Their silver illustrations on the height
And made the range their glaring satellite.

And like an alien mass
Beyond the confines of our heaving world,
Remote on seas of vapor wide unfurled
As the first shadows pass
And the first pallors of the dawn appear
It floats and overlooks the landscapes of our sphere.

Whiter its chalky facets glow,
Sharper the granite fences show
Under night's paling lamps;
The continental slopes pitch high
Into mid-heaven their jagged ramps,
The lunar cirques and craters lie
Under an irised sky.

Now through the eastern murk the sun
Breaks with his sultry rim
And unto him
Earth tilts its nebulous floor
Till more and more
The auroral couriers run
To lend yon cosmic battlements their crimson benison.

And lucid morning follows in their train;
Day's diamond beam
Like some crystalline inundation brims
The heaven's rims:
The wide inane
Glitters, and bathes the world as in some luminous dream.

The aerial snows indue
A silvery hue;
Metallic glamors fleet upon the slopes.

The spirit gropes
In nameless visions and inhuman tracts
Beyond earth's calms and storms,
The eyeballs seared and blind
With gazing on the eternal cataracts
Of light that pour upon the world of forms
From the exhaustless fountains of eternal mind.

NOVEMBER DUSK

THE forests leaned and tossed and swayed,
  The paths were matted with the leaves, —
But that tumultuous dusk bereaved
My heart of ill and dread.

The darkness drifted through the boughs
And overhead the still cloud raced,
And I recalled another place
And other vows.

The breath of some resistless might
Was in the pines, and their deep chant
Sang to the soul that powers haunt
The earth on such a night.

The leaves sustained their frenzied dance,
The crows fled on the flood of wind, —
And I was deaf and I was blind
In that dread circumstance.

For as the pines, my chords were thrilled,
And as the crows, my flight was borne,
And as the earth, my heights were stormed,
My heaven filled.

What mighty Pan was at his task?
What awful voice had spoken there?
His naked arm I saw him bare,
I saw the god unmask.

FIESOLE

REMEMBER—for too soon such hours take flight —
We dreamed a dream, and in our dream we stood
In silence by Fiesole at night

Above the old Etruscan rampart rude
By the Franciscan refuge; and we saw
The tranquil and the lavender evening brood

Upon its passing and review in awe
And tenderness the day's swift journey run;
We saw the last vermillion flares withdraw,

The young moon flash, the stars come one by one,
The livid Arno stagnate far below,
The lamps of Florence; and when day was done,

Through cypresses inked on the afterglow,
We heard the compline's golden tremors flow.

THE CITY OF MAN

A Florentine Reverie

TONIGHT this shell my soul long cast away
Unechoing from the chanting of the sea
Rang once again sonorous with the rhythm
Of the eternal breakers, resonant
And shaken with the uproar of the surf,
A rumor that usurped its every niche.
Its porcelain chamber held the Atlantic main,
And all the pulses of the eternal heart
Opening a way into this fragile brain,
Trembling in mortal veins, found tabernacle
For the primordial charities of God,
His ancient pities and august desires,
Within the narrow tenement of self
Whose walls expanding to the insurgent flow
Revealed the unfathomable depths within.

This night the mood was on me, won from brooding
And silent pacing by the Arno's bridges,
Notings of trudgers home, and knots of men
Boisterous in the wine shops, beggars, children,
And lovers pausing in the gloom of columns,
And awed perusal of the other world's
Foothold in this,—the bell-tower, incandescent,
Moving upon the horizon as I moved
Beside the huge star-blotting canopy
Of Brunelleschi, floating in the dusk,
And many a sleeping tower and pinnacle
Impassive o'er the dark roofs and the lights,
And the six bridges whose deep-shadowed spans
Stir premonitions of obscurer worlds
That lie beneath the piers of this we tread;

This night the mood was on me and I knew
The ruth and pity of a million years,
Entered the shadows of forgotten times,
Tasted the powers of the age to come;
Saw all the temples, all the spires and domes,
Saw all the forums and triumphal arches,
The aqueducts, the theatres, the quays,
Of all the peoples and of all the ages,
Rise on the sky in broken silhouette
Of ruin, or in pride of living use:
The various stages of a thousand kingdoms
Of past and present; some, ephemeral realms,
Hives whose forgotten murmur rose awhile
In wars obscure, in pomps and ritual orgy
And jubilation, and so died away
Bequeathing brooding pillars to the silence
That so succeeded; some, imperial lands
Whose galleys probed the gulfs of distant seas,
Whose legions woke the echoes of far isles,
And whose excitement in the blaze of day
Preoccupied the planet for an age,
Bridging oblivion with projected thought
And rolling back the muffling floods of death
With scaling dream and song of stellar span;
Whose tumult in the silence of the sky,
Whose order in the gardens of the sun
No less was gulfed in peace, to leave its stones
Gouged with the indecipherable runes
Of vanished art, the signature of Man,
Hieroglyphs of the logos. And I saw
Besides these, occupying earth's horizons,
The towers around which teem in myriads
The living, in far corners of the earth,
Or here at hand, standing like lighthouses

Above the generations as they surge, —
The stages of the peoples, streets and marts,
Bastions and fortresses and masonries,
Whereto acceding from the mysterious ports
Of birth, uncounted souls take up their place,
Appropriating there with tower and spire
The attachments of their forebears and their faiths,
To love and hate, traffic and breed and die,
Ruled by the ascendency of heritage
In their small cosmos, and from birth to death
Without a glance turned on the aghast abyss
Of thought, nor ever hearkening
To the appalling roaring of the waters
Risen in flood beneath the piers of day.

The ruth and pity of a million years
Spoke in my heart. I knew the voice was God's
Articulate in the handiwork of man
Refined by time, whereby the Duomo globe,
The Giotto apparition, and the spears
Of thought that rose around me, seemed to rise
Out of the heart's core of humanity
Anonymously speaking from the dead,
Creative in its travail and divine
And bearing witness to its ground in God.
The myriads groping through the restricted course
Of their swift days, and each one baited on
Each in his place by life's sufficient lures
To lift the load of days and in hot blood
To meet the knives of life insensible
Through passion, found about these stones
That lie today in ruins, those same faiths
And loyalties which won their hearts to toil,
To strife, and so to life. Unconsciously

Building according to their thirst for life
They gave to God himself a voice in clay
Which still speaks to us though the builders sleep.

No less the eternal spirit draws us on
Through lures proportionate to our pilgrim souls —
Objects but little nobler than the fees
And guerdons of the battle-games of old,
Yet round which that within the heart of man
Which is divine casts glamor not of earth —
To self-creation in the toils of action
And to the praise of God in self-abandon.
From our unconscious deed when we are gone
And others like us for a thousand years,
Doubt not that there emerges and survives
A coral structure from our minute lives
Which towering ever as the flood recedes
And sanctified by time shall tell the races
Of other epochs that our submerged days
And straitened thought, through faith and toil and blood,
Yet drew on God who working o'er our heads
Transmuted imperfection into art
And built up glory from relinquished dreams
And made of clay memorial to stilled prayer,
Giving our silted graves power in the light,
Our smothered outcries voice in the upper air.

Yet all our structures shall be razed, nor shall
Their rest one stone upon another placed
By our primeval days, for in the time
Of consummation when the eternal Breath
Exalts the imaginations of our kind
And fires the conceits whereby men build,
Then shall men fashion habitations such

That all our most ethereal fanes shall seem
But lead to gold or mire to alabaster;
Then cities shall arise whose contours sweep
Harmonious with the lineaments of heaven,
Proportionate to nature, and of hues
That merge with the suffused tints of dawn;
Where an elated race, their plagues dispelled,
Their demons exorcised, shall crown our dearth.
In their deep hearts our tears and joys shall live
As in their gleaming domes and monuments
The themes and motives of our humbler shafts:
Our hopes and hungers flowering in their crafts.
So shall the sun rise on a gracious earth
And the wide rumor of the sons of men
Be all seraphic at its going down,
And moons soar over guileless continents.

18274379R00062

Made in the USA
San Bernardino, CA
07 January 2015